# *What*
# JESUS
## *Says About It*

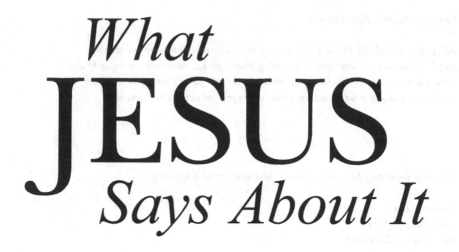

# *What*
# JESUS
## *Says About It*

## BREN DANIELS

# WHAT JESUS SAYS ABOUT IT

*iUniverse books may be ordered through booksellers or by contacting:*

*iUniverse LLC*
*1663 Liberty Drive*
*Bloomington, IN 47403*
*www.iuniverse.com*
*1-800-Authors (1-800-288-4677)*

*ISBN: 978-1-4917-3982-2 (sc)*
*ISBN: 978-1-4917-3984-6 (hc)*
*ISBN: 978-1-4917-3983-9 (e)*

*Printed in the United States of America.*

*iUniverse rev. date: 08/19/2014*

# Contents

## Encouragement

## Faithful

## Family

## Forgive

## Friend

## Humble

## Joy

## Love

## Test

## Trust

## Victory

# 1

## *Being Tempted By The Devil And Knowing You Already Passed The Test*

—◦⑨◦—

Although you're being tempted, and although your being tried. Always remember your tests you have had. So when the devil tries to bring it up again, you can say "Uh uh, devil. I have passed that test. You need to try something else. Because I have passed that test. You got to talk back to the devil when he starts talking to you. Know who you are in Christ. Know your authority that God has given you, and use it on the enemy. When he comes against you to tempt you once again. Know that you have gotten the victory through Christ Jesus.

# 2

## Don't Let the Devil Dictate How You Act

—⚬𝔖⚬—

The devil is just like a company you have been with before. You quit using the company and you were such a faithful customer, and they were making a lot of money off you. So they kept calling you, writing letters to you, and trying to win you back. That's how the devil works. He always trying to tempt you to get you to fall back in sin. But don' t let the devil dictate how you act. You may have let him stop you from going to Church, and someone came by that day, and you decided not to go because, you had company; your stocking tore right before Church; and you felt you didn't have the right dress. But from now on tell the devil. "Oh! No devil, I have passed that test, and I'm going on." That's in the past, those excuses you keep trying to bring back: I dictate how my actions are. In stopping me from going on to do the things of God. You no longer can dictate how I act. Though you keep trying to bring the same things up to stop me from going to Church, or praying, or fasting, or studying, the Word of God. Say," Uh, Uh, devil no more.

I've passed that test. You know longer can dictate how I act.

# A Word To the Wise

—⁓⟋§⟍⁓—

Be ye steadfast, unmovable, always abounding in the work of the Lord. For your labor will never be in vain for the Lord. God will always reward you for your work. So never get weary in well-doing. You will surely reap if you faint not. And always remember what you went through to stay strong in the Lord. The fasting, praying, and the reading God's word. Obeying God and how you got treated for obeying God. So if you can look back over your life and remember your trials and testing you won't so easily give up. Because what you invested in you won't give up without a fight. So, keep the faith, and keep the fight to stay strong in the Lord everyday for the rest of your life.

# Your Labor Is not In Vain

Although you minister to people and speak of God words. Your labor is not in vain, though you tell God is love, for he, who show love is of God. Your labor is not in vain, though you give a smile, and tell there's hope Your labor is not in vain, though you greet people with hugs and with kisses. Your labor is not in vain, though you go through trial, and though you go through test. Your labor is not in vain, and to sum it up and tell you all. For God hears and sees what you do. For he is not unrighteous to forget your good works that you do. Your labor is not in vain, for he is faithful that promise. Your labor is not in vain, so what you're doing, keep doing-ministering, witnessing, telling of God goodness, telling there's hope. For one day you will be rewarded. For your labor is not in vain.

# 5

## Someone Who Will Never Fail You

There's one person in the whole wide world who will never fail you. He will never hurt you, lie on you, never cheat on you, never abuse you, never talk about you, and never use you or never let you down; Never cause you hurt, harm, or pain. He will never cause your heart to hurt. He will never cause you pain. He will never cause tears to run down your face. He will always be around. He will never let you down. He will never treat you like other people. He won't ever fail you. He will do you good and not evil all the days of your life. For if disappointments come, let down come, and they will come, you will have him number one. And you will know you will be able to stand. For if your hand is in Jesus hand. You will always be able to stand. As long as you keep Jesus number one in your life. You will always be all right, because he will never leave you or ever forsake you. Most of all, he will never fail you. Amen

# Caring Is Sharing

—⦿—

We shouldn't have to wait just for Christmas time, Easter time or family reunion time to come together. Family should be close throughout the year. Even if it's a phone call to say I am thinking of you. Or just a card to say you're on my mind. We should be close throughout the year. Even if it's a phone call to say I am thinking of you, Or just a card to say you're on my mind. We should care for each other throughout the year, Showing love, joy, and concernment. Family should be special. Family should stick together. Not just in bad times, but in good times. Family should come together. So after this time of excitement and joy of being together, Remember one thing, family should always stick together.

# God Is The Apple of My Eye

—⟶ჹ⟵—

Have you ever had an apple that was red and delicious? Have you ever had a pear which was very delicious? You ever had a grape which was very great? You ever had a plum which is good all the time? You ever had a peach which was delicious to eat: Well, I have a God who is as delicious as an apple. I have a friend who is very good to the end. I have a Father who is always caring for me everyday. I have a friend who is closer than anyone could be to me. I have a helper who is always there to help me along the way. My apple of my eye is God. He is as peachy as can be. He is as great as a grape and good as a plum. He is my God and he is very good to me. To serve him is an honor and I am happy as can be. I thank God for giving me all these good things. Which is truly good for me. That's why I am naming fruit because he is as fresh, gracious, merciful, loving, kind, righteous. He is all these and much much more to me. Fruit can't really begin to compare to him. These are just some fruits to share with you. Because I love my friend. And he's everything to me. The fruit is just a way of expressing myself. For what God is to me.

He is as fresh as sunlight, he is bright as a morning star. He is my God and he it is that keeps me doing all right. I love my bright and morning star. And most of all, I love the apple of my eye. Jesus, God the Father, and Precious Holy Spirit. For they are the apple of my eye.

# Maintaining Your Integrity

You are going to go through trials and test. And you will be disappointed and let down. You may have heartaches and pain. But one thing you have got to always remember. That you are maintaining your integrity for Jesus. If you remember that you will be honest to God and tell him your true feelings. If it's lust you feel, tell Jesus. If it's disappointments you feel, tell Jesus. If it's abuse you feel, tell Jesus. Whatever the situation may be, talk to Jesus about it. Whatever the test may be, talk to Jesus about it. Then he can help you. You have to call on God in sincerity and truth, And tell God you don't want to do anything, to mess your relationship up with him. Tell Jesus you don't want to hurt him. You don't want to backslide. You don't want to be like others. Who have said I once had that joy of the Lord. But obstacles came in my life. And I forgot about maintaining my integrity. Because of the situation, I did evil for evil. Or I got back at them because they hurt me. Or what I done, I felt like doing. Or make excuses for their sins. Instead of them saying I didn't maintain my integrity. You see satan will send someone when you're being tested, and you have been done wrong. Just to get you to do wrong as well. See it's not so much as what they're done to you. But he wants to get you to mess up with God. See, he knows what you have going on with God just as much as you do. So that's why he's trying in to get you to mess up, while you're being tested. He wants to come back and tempt you. But don't fall for his lies. And his tempts, he tries to send your way. Remember all your praying, fasting, studying, going to Bible study, Prayer, Church ( both services on Sunday). Remember all your witnessing, all the people you have told about God. Remember all that you have done. And what you work hard to get, too. You won't so easily give it up for anyone, So always go back to remembering how you have fought the good fight of faith. And held on to God and you won't so easily give it up for anyone, so remember the next time your being tried and tested. Remember you have to maintain your integrity for the cause of Christ And never to shame his name. Then you won't so easily mess up. When you look back on how God kept you all these years. You will continue to maintain your integrity, for God is near. And he will help you. If you are sincere and you don't want to mess up your relationship with him. He can keep you if you don't want to mess up. He's a keeper if you want to be kept. Maintaining your integrity for the cause of Christ. Amen

# 9

## *Encouraging*

---◦§◦---

Change your way of thinking, change your way of mind, if you allow God to do it for you. You will not fear at times. Trouble will come your way. But it is so easy to pray, If you trust God to lead your way. You can never go wrong any day. What you confess with your mouth you make happen. Words are powerful. But if you speak positive in a negative situation good always overcomes evil. You can never lose for being positive. You can never lose for being right. Speak over your day everyday and always pray. For prayer changes things Prayer also changes you. If you stay in the presence of God. He will keep you in fullness of joy. He will keep you in safety. So be encourage and trust the only living true God. For Jesus is the only way to go. So everyday you must pray, and you can determine through prayer how you will spend everyday. So confess your day and let Jesus lead your way. He will lead you and you will have a successful day everyday if you will only pray.

# 10

## *Here's A Poem Just For You*

—⟡—

I hope by now after reading this poem, you know who I am. Although I'm gone, I'm still near remember my smiles and my cheers. Never feel lonely or dismayed, for the Lord thy God, he's with you everyday when you put your trust in him, When you believe in him, He will assure you he's always around. So don't ever feel down or ever feel like something is to hard, for God will never put no more on you then you can bear. So smile each and everyday, because it's a blessing to see another day. Remember my smiles along the way. And remember how excited I get just to express the love of God to you all. Everyday thru smiles and words of cheer. Because Jesus lives in me I am happy throughout the year.

## 11

## Being Real In All That You Do For Christ

—⟶∽ஞ∽⟵—

You can be real in what you say. You can be real in what you do. It just all depends on you. Why take the time to fake it? When you can be real and make it. The time you take to pretend is time you can use to be real within. You're going to face things when you're Saved. But you're going to face things when you're not saved. So don't you think you would be better off to go through things when you're Saved. To know you have a helper in time of need? So put your trust in Jesus and be real with all you can be. For never ashaming God's name, you shouldn't want to do Because God is so real indeed. And God has been really good to you.

# 12

## It's Already Done

When you pray and you trust in the Lord, it's already done. When you know your prayer's been heard, it's already done, So then all you got to do is have the confidence in the prayer you have prayed it's already done, just trust the Lord and always remember that the Lord's ear is open to a righteous person prayer. And remember a fervent prayer of a righteous man availeth much. So when you pray from your heart with all your mind, body, soul, and everything within you. God hears a sincere prayer, and he will answer, because he is the answer. So trust God and don't worry about how, when, where, and how long but just know he is well able to fix any and every situation you may face and to say all that God is well able to supply all of your needs and above your needs. It's already done.

## 13

## *Don't Point Fingers: It Could Hurt*

—◦§◦—

If you see someone hurting even in pain, don't point fingers, it could hurt, you say no I would never do that, if I saw someone hurting. Well why when you see someone on drugs, you talk about them or you see someone smoking, you condemn them or you see someone drinking alcohol you put them down, or found in adultery you point fingers. You're still hurting someone you may say I'm not pointing fingers, it's the truth, well what's in your life that your doing wrong that know one sees, for God sees all things that you do, why not pray for them instead of talking about them? Don't point fingers, it could hurt you want mercy you must also show mercy don't point fingers, it could hurt. Even Jesus showed compasssion on people don't point fingers, it could hurt. So pray for people witness to people encourage people, love people, comfort people, tell people there's hope,. Because when you point your finger the point always come back to you, and the point does hurt.

# 14

## *Why Do You Complain?*

—◦⟨ჟ⟩◦—

Remember where you came from and where you are at. Why do you complain? Remember when you had nothing and now that you know me you have something. Why do you complain? I never failed you or left you when troubles came. Why do you complain? Maybe I didn't come when you wanted me to but I was never late, I was always on time. Why do you complain? You say you want to be used by me but why do you complain? Words are easy to say. Even wanting to is also easy to think, but when you really put what you say to action. That's when it means something Why do you complain? Quit complaining, quit murmuring, quit being bitter, quit being mean, quit being unthankful, and most of all, quit forgetting how good I have been to you. Remember where I brought you from and now where you are, I don't change I still love you the same so why do you still complain?

# 15

## Jesus Is The Way

—◦✎◦—

The only way to go, Jesus is the way, he is the one to know. Jesus is the way, he will be a true friend, Jesus is the way. He will never betray you. Jesus is the way. He will always be there for you, Jesus is the way, to help you out in time of need. Jesus is the way he won't lie on you Jesus is the way, he won't talk about you, he won't backstab you, he won't say he say she say. Jesus is the way, he will be a friend that sticks closer than a brother Jesus is the way, he won't be envious of you Jesus is the way. He won't be jealous of you Jesus is the way. He won't pretend to be a friend, Jesus is the way, He knows how to keep a secret Jesus is the way, then fix it just for you Jesus is the way, he will be a dear friend to you, until the very end, that's true, I know Jesus is the way.

# 16

## My Friend

—⁓⟆⁓—

People say they are your friend. Do you know what a friend is? A friend is someone who love you unconditionally. To tell you just a few things about a friend. A friend is someone who cares, someone who is always there. Someone who will be there in time of need. Someone to cry with, someone to laugh with, someone to pick you up when you're down, someone to comfort you when you need a hug, someone to say it will get better indeed, someone to say I' ll be here. I will never leave someone who will be there to the end. Someone who keeps his word. Someone you can trust someone you know someone you have confidence in, someone who loves you whether you're rich or poor. And need not I say more, that someone that I know his name is Jesus and there's no one else I know, these are just a few things to describe my friend. I just wanted you to know he's the one whom you can trust to the very end. If you want to know my friend. You can find him in reading his word and his word is the Holy Bible. He's my friend, he's my true friend. And there's no other.

## 17

## *Do As You Say*

People love to tell their children things to do, but do they also do as they say to do. They tell their children don't do this or don't do that. Do as you say. They say I don't want you lying. Do as you say. They say I don't want you cheating. Do as you say. They say I want you to do what's right. Do as you say. You get mad when they don't be strong in things that happen. Well, look at yourself. You tell them don't lie, don't cheat, do what's right, and make Mommy proud. But then you also say Mommy can do this, but you can't do this because mommy is grown,. Well, if you want them to do what's right. You must first set and example for them, and not just tell them. What you expect but you must also do as you say.

# You Say You're Saved; Where Is The Evidence?

~ॐ~

You go around saying you're saved. Where is the evidence? You come to Church on Sunday sometimes, even to both services. Where is the evidence? You come to Wednesday night Bible Study, Where is the evidence? You even come to Friday night prayer. Where is the evidence? Even when the Pastor calls other services such as Prayer a whole week, do not watch TV a whole month, and for the Church to go on a fast, but I still don't see any evidence. If you are in my presence this much, there should be a change. If not, you need to come back to the altar. All the power I'm sending out, yet you're not receiving it. There's no such excuse why there shouldn't be evidence of you being Saved. You know too much truth, yet you act like you don't know how to be Saved. Take a look at yourself and ask your own self a question, is there any real evidence of me being Saved?

# You Can't Serve God And Mammon Too

You can't do what the world do, and say you're Saved. You can't go the same places the world goes to, and say you're Saved. You can't serve God and mammon, too. You can't go to dances. You can't tell lies, steal, false witness, just to name a few. And say you're Saved. What will the world say if you're doing the same things they are. What need they may feel, they need to get Saved. When you say you're Saved, but yet you do the same things they do. There should be a difference. There's a difference between clean and unclean. So you need to think about who you're going to serve. You either going to hate one and love the other. Are you going to cleave to one, and despise the other. So you choose whom this day you're going to serve. Because when you're lukewarm God will spue you out of his mouth. So, who will you serve, God or mammon?

# 20

## How Far Will You Go For Jesus?

You say with your mouth. "I love him" but yet your action show different. You say I'll praise him, but you're ashamed. You say you love the Saints, but yet you talk about them. You say, I'll go where you want me to Lord, but yet you complain. You say, I'll do what you say, but if it's not what you want to do you're not happy. But in it all, you say you will go where Jesus want you to, but you lie, you talk about people, you complain, you're not even full of joy. You're even ashamed at times of his name. So, how far will you go for Jesus? Take a look at yourself. And see if that's just words, or if your words and action means the same. For God already know just how far you will go for his name. So don't fool yourself. For God sees your action and hears your words. So be careful what you say, and also what you do. Because it will show God just how far you will go in things you say and do.

## 21

### Remember Me

———ↄଵↄ———

When you were going through, I was there. When the storms were coming. I was there. When you were in trouble. I was there. When no one could help you. I was there. When people mistreated you. I was there. When you cried, I was there. When you thought that there was no hope, I was there, Now that everything is okay, You have forgotten how I delivered you in trouble times. Take not for granted, I was there. Because, sure enough, there will be a next time. And you will be calling for me to deliver you and you will want me to be also there. I love you and I want to be there. So remember me in good times and bad times. For I will never leave you or ever forsake you. I will always be there.

# 22

## Cast Your Cares On Me

—⟡—

In my words I said cast all your cares on me, for I care for you. Why do you worry? Why do you cry? Why do you miss sleep? I don't understand why. You say you trust me, you say you know I care. But yet you carry your burdens around as though I'm not there. When things are going wrong, you forget who I am. You say you know I love you, but yet you forget my name. When troubles come your way, you won't even try to pray. You let the devil beat you up. As though you have no power that I have given you. If you say I'm your Father, don't you know I care. If you stomp your toe, even that matters. So remember when you're going through and you feel that your heart is burden. Remember I am that I am and I will help you. When you're in trouble I love you and I care, So when you're going through know that I am always there.

# 23

## Why Let The Devil Beat You Up Before Coming To God?

———— ✦ ————

Why wait until you're going through to realize you need God? Why do you have to get beat up from the devil to want to change, or almost get killed or loose a leg, break your neck, hurt your back, get in a wheel chair or be hospitalized, for a storm to come, or even to be bombed, to call on Jesus. Everyone seems to know how to pray when trouble comes their way. Don't you think it's easier to already always pray. And know God as being the only true way? So when trouble comes, and one day it will, You will already know that God will see you through. You won't have to say, Lord if you help me! I'll go to Church or give God false petitions. Because after God has healed you and have had mercy on you, You so easily forget what state you were in. So know the Lord without having to go through something. Love him just for him loving you. He gave you life. He gave you a chance to get it right. So do it! And live because if you don't give him your life, you shall surely die. For the devil will never give up the fight. But God will help you to stay alive. If you will let him help you live your life.

# When You Can Do, And Won't Do

So many people complain about things that they can't do. But what about the things you can do? There are some people who love the Lord with all their heart, soul, body, mind, and everything that is within them. But what about those who confess with their mouth? But their hearts are far from loving God. To love God you must show God. Some people can go whenever they want to, with nothing stopping them. Then others have so many things they have to do, but yet they still try to do what's right according to what God says to do. You who are blessed to go, come freely as you will. You must know that you can really do all that God requires you. Not making excuses for those who have other things to attend. The whole point in writing this poem. Is to say you can go to Church, Bible Study, Prayer, and other Churches following the Pastor, a week of Prayer, when the Pastor calls it. Go, come, with your whole heart. For there are some who go through a lot. Yet even hurt, when they can't do what God says to do right then, because there are things that seem to always try to stop them. So what is your excuse? Why don't you do what God say? Without complaining when you can do just what he wants you to do.

# 25

## *What A Friend*

—◦§◦—

Although I'm not there, I am near. In order to have a friend, you must first be a friend. Friends are forever if they are true. It doesn't matter where you go or what you do. A true friend will always be around. It doesn't matter how far the distance. They're still where they can be found. I will miss you, but I know you have to go. But there's one friend I know, he will always be near. His name is Jesus and he's a friend that will stick closer than a brother. If ever you need a Friend and I'm not around. Where you can call me or need someone to depend on. Jesus line is never busy. He neither sleeps nor slumbers. He doesn't have call waiting, or even a busy signal. If you call on him, he will be there. In whatever you do, make him your friend. And he will always be there to see you through.

# Why Wait Until You Get In Trouble To Call On Jesus?

⟶ ✦ ⟵

When you can know God without going through, you're blessed. When you can know him without something happening to you you're blessed. A lot of things you wouldn't experience if you know him. You take the hard way because if it doesn't edify Christ it will lead you to destruction. So why go the hard way? When you can avoid a lot of things if you will just get Saved. Being Saved is an honor. Being saved is a joy. Being Saved is much more than just being Saved. You have a keeper, you have a Saviour, you have a healer, you have a way maker, and much, much more. So why struggle in life when you don't have to? Because when you don't know God, you will go through many things. And remember only what you do for Christ will last. So don't wait until trouble come to call on him. Because one day you might, and it might be too late.

## 27

### Pressing My Way Toward The Things Of God

—⟨𝔖⟩—

Sometimes trials may come. Sometimes tribulation too. But you can't give up no matter how hard it gets. You have to press your way toward the things of God: You have to press your way toward the mark of the prize of the high calling in Christ Jesus. Through storms of life. Through tests you face daily. Even when you're afraid you can't give up. For Jesus is able to secure you in all that you face in life. Even as Jesus was tempted, so should we be as well. But he passed every test he had. And so can we as well, If we trust in God in all that we do. He will be there just for us too. So press on each and every day and trust God to know with confidence that he will lead you the way. So get anchor in God, so that you won't give up. Because test will surely come. But if you trust God, you will know he will be there for you in all that you do.

## Praying Always

Men ought to always pray and not faint. You wonder why you have know joy? Do you pray? You wonder why you stay depress? Do you pray? You wonder why you can't handle things that happen in your life? Do you pray? You wonder why the devil keep messing with you? Do you pray? You must realize you can't survive without praying. You can't survive without Jesus. You can't defeat the devil in your power are strength, because you have none. You can't do anything without Jesus. So pray each and everyday so when things come your way. You will be able to stand, because you never know when your going to go through. But if you pray you will be able to handle anything that comes your way, because Jesus will fight just for you when you pray.

## 29

### Storing Up, And Putting Your Time In

—⚬⟿⚬—

Put your time in. Your never know when you're going to need it. But if you have put your time in and you are stored up. When troubles come your way you will just know how to pray. You won't be discouraged. You won't even be afraid, for you will know the hand of God will help you along the way. For as the ant stores up in the summer, preparing for winter. So should you at all times. So that when troubles come you will be able to handle it knowing that Jesus will lead your way. So store up now, for the time is at hand. So when problems come, you will be able to stand. Yes, it might hurt you and you might even have to cry, but because you know Jesus is there for you. You will already know how it will come out. So put your time in while everything is okay. So when you face trial in life. You will know just how to pray. Because you had been praying all along and you will already be strong. So put your time in each and every day. So that you will have the assurance that when test come Jesus will help you along the way.

# How Can You Be Ashamed of God?

When you were in the world and you were going through. God was still being good to you. Even now that you're Saved you face trials and tribulation, how can you be ashamed? When you were going through, you weren't ashamed to call on his name. When you were hurting and needed help. You wasn't ashamed to call on his name. When you were in trouble, and didn't know how you was going to make it out of the situation, you weren't ashamed of his name. And look where God has brought you from, and now where you are. How can you be ashamed of his name? How can you be ashamed to talk about him? How can you be ashamed to worship and praise him? How can you not talk about him everywhere you go? Any place can be the right place. You just have to have the mind that your going to do what Jesus says. No matter what it cost you. For he didn't mind doing it for you. So count it up and know who really paid the price, it was Jesus Christ, the Son of the Most High God. So remember next time you're ashamed, remember who name will always be the same. Though you go through trials, tribulation, test, famine, pestilence, and many more, remember Jesus name will always be the same. So people don't be ashamed of his glorious name.

# Men Being The Men God Wants Them To Be

Men should take their stand. Men should be what God want them to be. To be loving, to be kind, to be helpful in times of need. To cheer someone on in their time of need. Men need to be just what God wants them to be, Not to please man, but to please God. Men need to take a stand. God wants you to be the head and not the tail. The leader and not the follower. The loving husband and not the boss. But to show that God is in you in everything you do. To be the man God wants you to be without pride, without shame, without taking God glory, and uplifting your name,. Jesus wants you to be free. He wants you to be just what he wants you to be. So surrender your heart and mind and bow down to Jesus and say I give you my heart, soul, body, and mind.

# 32

## Staying Prayed Up

Stay prayed up at all times because you never know when it's your time. To face tests in life, to face trials that come by, but if you prayed up, you will be able to stand what comes up. Things that get you down you won't walk around with a frown. You will know, no matter what you face. You will know Jesus will help you through the test. Praying all the time will help you stay in control. You won't ever lose what God has given you through things you've heard. So stay prayed up at all time. So when you go through things in life, you will know Jesus is around.

# 33

## Loving The Saints

—⟋ҩ⟍—

We suppose to especially love those who are in the house hold of faith. We're supposed to love them anyway, whether they are rich or poor, black or white, It doesn't matter what their nationality is. We're suppose to love them anyhow. We need to encourage each other along the way because there's test we all must face. But when we encourage each other in their time of need, then Jesus will touch someone heart when we are in need. Do unto others the way you would have them do to you. Remembering what you do will come back to you. So be kind one to another, stay in hope and in faith, encouraging each other.

# *Helping God People*

Those that be of the house of God especially are the ones we should help. Why talk about your brother are sister in Christ. Or be jealous or envious of how they are doing? You should cheer them on and be happy for them. Not saying things to condemn. Your words should be pleasant. They should be sweet. Especially for those who is of the house of faith whom you meet. Why not help them instead of cursing them? Why not bless them instead of hurting them? You should love them as you love yourself. Because the love God has for them-he cares for them as well. So help God children when they are in need. Bless them and you will succeed. To do what's right you should want to do. Because you're doing it right before God's eye sight, And because it's the right thing to do.

# Helping One Another

When your brother or sister is in need. Help them will you please. Don't be too proud to help out knowing that one day it could be you that need helped out. In need of healing, in need of delivering, in need of hope, in need of care. Because one day you will want things to be fair. So help one another while you can. For some day, you will want someone praying for you. To do unto you the things that you need them to do. So help out why you can don't put off tomorrow what's already in your hand.

# 36

## Only The Pure In Heart Shall See God

~ຣ~

When you come to God, you have to come to him in realness. You have to come to God with a pure heart. Not bitter in your spirit, Not angry with someone, Not complaining, Not coming to God like he owes you something. For God owes you nothing, but you should feel you owe him. Jesus died for us and rose again so that we would be free from sin. So because of Jesus we have eternal life. Through him and by him only can our sins be forgiven. So in order for us to see God, we have to be free from sin. Because without holiness we will not see God. So stay humble in your spirit, very repentive because only the pure in heart shall see God.

# Keep Jesus Your Main Line

—⊸⟲⊶—

When you have Jesus he's the only line you need. Not call waiting or third party line or even personal to personal, but when you have him as your main line. You don't need an operator to put you through. Or even an answering computer to talk to you to tell you what numbers to put in first. But when the number you are dialing is direct, that is when your calling heaven. All you need to do is say "Jesus" and that immediately puts you in the presence of God. So don't wait until things happen in your life to try to get in touch with Jesus. Keep him as your main line and he will always be there right in time, and you won't ever have to hear another voice because the only voice you will need will be Jesus. And his line will always be clear for you in times of need. So keep him as your main line. And you will succeed.

# 38

## *Filled With The Holy Ghost*

—⟨§⟩—

Are you filled with the Holy Ghost? Are you filled with things that don't make a difference? Being filled with the Holy Ghost is power-boldness, speaking with authority, humble in the spirit, very repentive, being convicted when you're doing wrong. Not being ashamed to talk about Jesus. Encouraging, Loving, Kind, Faithful, just to name a few. So are these pertaining to the things you say and do. Words are so easily to say, but actions makes the difference. So check your life are you powerful in the Lord? Or are you powerless? Are you bitter or are you sweet? If not go back to the altar and ask Jesus to fill you with the Holy Ghost. Because if you're not like this you won't be able to survive satan's defeats.

# There's Nothing New Under The Sun

~·§·~

In my words I say there's nothing new under the sun, There's nothing covered won't be uncovered. You can't hide, you can't cheat, for the same things you're doing. Are things that were before you came to be. You think it's new, but yet it's old. And if it don't edify the Lord, you will soon be destroyed, the devil doesn't change: he's still the same. What he did yesterday, he's doing also today. But Glory be to Jesus, for he says in his Word, he's God and he changes not. So what your going through some one was going through yesterday. It was before your time and now it's trying to play with your mind. So trust the Lord Jesus Christ to lead your way. For what he helped you with before when you were going through. He will still help you with what your going through today. For there's nothing new under the sun, because God the Lord Jesus has already won.

# 40

## Put On The Whole Armor of God

―❦―

Put on the whole armor of God while it is day. For the night will come and you will be ready for it. You will shine forth, bright in the darkness of the night. For God Glory will overtake you. He will Minister to you in the mist of the night. Though storms of life might pass you by, though testing times is near, you will know that your true Saviour is near. He's the only one who can help you in storms of life. He can calm the storm and say peace be still. Even the wind and waves obey him. Even the rocks cry out before him so trust in God in all that you do. Put on the whole armor of God and know that he will be there for you.

# 41

## Praise Him All People

—⟡—

When you praise God in realness, God inhabits your praise. When you praise him from the heart, that's when your blessing will start. God loves to see you praise him. God loves to see you dance. It makes him proud and happy to see you bless his name. God wish to bless you, but you have to get a spirit of praise. Because real praise moves God. Real praise he loves it. So next time you're in Church praising God, or at home, or on your job, or just riding in your car, remember whatever you do unto God. Let it be form the heart.

# 42

## Be Kind One To Another

~⌘~

In my words I say do unto others as you would have them do unto you. How you want to be treated? You want to be treated kind. You want to be treated nice. Think about how you treat others. See if it's nice. You want people to smile at you. Think about it, are you smiling back? You want someone to laugh with you. Are you laughing back? What you do to any one it will come back to you. So make sure when you plant a seed, make sure it's one you want to come back. How you treat some one will determine how you get treated back. So be kind one to another, and the same kindness you give it will come back to you and it will be real. And it will be the same kindness you gave to another.

# 43

## Staying In The Spirit

—◦§◦—

For I know the spirit is willing, but the flesh is weak, but that's know excuse to be in defeat. For I have given you power and also said be strong in the Lord. So how come you keep losing when you're strong? I have already paid the price. Why do you keep hurting? You don't have to because I have already given my life. Stay in the spirit. Do not be carnal because when you do, you will feel very vulnerable. I love you and I will help you. That's why I sent my spirit to help you along the way. So that you would never be defeated at the end of any day.

# 44

## *Allowing Jesus To Be Real*

—⚶—

You don't have to fake it to make it. You can be real in anything you say and feel. There's nothing fake about me in everything I do. I wish to set you free. The price has already been paid. Why are you dismayed? Even after you say you have prayed. When you pray in sincerity and you pray in truth, I unlock doors that has been closed to you. There's nothing I can't fix, there's nothing hard for me. When you allow me to be real, that is when I can set you free. Troubles will come your way, but it's so easy to pray. If you allow me to be God, I will fix it for you today.

# 45

## Allow Jesus To Keep You

—⟡—

If you want to be kept, I'm able to keep you. If you want me to be the head of your life. I am able to keep you. In order for me to keep you, you have to allow me too. I won't force myself on you. For I am love, I am gracious, I am kind, I am forgiving, but I'm not forcible. I don't take what I want; I give you a choice. So if you want me to guide your life, you have to let me direct your path. And acknowledge me in all your ways. And then I will order all your steps in my word. If you will only allow me to keep you by reading my word.

## 46

# Allowing Jesus To Shape You, Mold You, To Be What He Wants You To Be

❧

If you allow me to mold you to be what I want you to be, you will see there's nothing hard for me. I can harden a heart, I can soften a heart, but if you want me to make you, you have to allow me to start. I won't force myself on you. I won't try to make you change. I'll let you make that decision. So if you turn out wrong, and you will if you don't let me guide you. To do the work I want to do. To make you just what I want you to be. To make you happy and set you free. I will never fail you, or even leave you. I will always be there to encourage, you, so allow me to set you free and then only can I make you to be just what I want you to be.

# 47

## Being Used By God

If you want to be used by God, you must first humble yourself. You can't be with pride. You can't be with shame. You can't try to take God's glory and uplift your name. You must stay in the spirit; You must stay in truth that's the only way God can tell you what to do. You have to be bold, you have to be sincere. That's the only way you can hear him clear. You can't be bitter. You can't be unforgiving. You will have to stay Holy so that you can say what God mean. You will have some test when your doing what God say. But you must remember he will guide you along the way. He will never leave you alone. He will never let you fear. For he will assure you, his presence is very near so trust God in all you do, because he's your keeper and he will be there just for you.

# 48

## There's Power In The Name Of Jesus

~⑨~

Even the rocks cry out to Jesus. Even the rocks praise Jesus. The power of his name is mighty. The power of his name is life. The power of his name is hope. The power of his name is healing. The power of his name is delivering. The power of his name is joy. The power of his name is peace. The power of his name is Salvation. And just to name a few, because there's so many words that I could write to express the power of the mighty name of Jesus to you. If you call on him in any situation you may be facing. He's not too busy to hear your cry. You must come in sincerity. You must come in truth because when you come with a pure heart. Jesus can give you an answer just for you. So call on his name. I tell you it won't be in vain. He never lost a battle; he never lost a test. So give what you're going through to Jesus and let him handle the rest.

# 49

## What You Ask God In Faith

—⟊—

What you ask God believing he's able to do. You just have to believe what you're asking that he's able to do. Without faith, it's impossible to please God. But to have faith, all things are possible to him that believes. When you come to God. You have to know he is a rewarder of them who diligently seek him. And he is help in their time of need. For he says, "I will deliver you because you trust in me. And because you believe in me, I will set you free." So have faith in my words and quote my scriptures. And my words that you have heard. When you're in need, get in faith and believe I'm able to do exactly what you believe. In faith, I'll move, in faith I'll do what you ask, but first you have to know I will before you ask.

# 50

## Seeing The Unseen

—⟡—

The devil will paint you a pretty picture. He will try to make things look nice. But if it doesn't edify God, you will be lost. You need to see the unseen, because what's in the dark will sooner or later come to the light. You might even get by, but you won't get away. What ever you're doing, it will catch up with you one day. So see if what you're doing if it's not good, it will come to an end real soon. Things may go well for a while, but if it's not toward God, You will sure enough not survive. So open up your eyes and see the truth that the devil is setting you up just to kill you. But if you open up your eyes and let Jesus be your guide, then you will surely enough have a chance to survive.

# 51

## Staying Prayerful

—◦§◦—

Stay in the spirit. Stay in truth. For prayer will be a keeper to carry you through, so stay prayerful at all times. So when you need Jesus, you will know he's around. He will always be there in the mist of prayer. He will guide you and give you what to say. He will teach you many things in prayer if you pray. He will show you how to live day by day. So stay in tune to Jesus everyday. So that he will teach you many things and tell you just how to pray. For we don't pray as we ought to say God word, but the spirit himself maketh intercession for us. So that God will be there in time of need. To tell us what to do so that we can be free.

# 52

## In '98

~§~

In 1998, when you go through a trial and when you go through a test remember, God is there. He will help you out. Don't get frustrated. Don't give up. God is making you to be the best. It's through weakness you are made strong. So what ever your going through, only remember God has planned no defeats for you. He will bring you out if you depend totally on him. So when your going through trials and when your going through tests keep a smile, for God knows what's best. And he's making you to be what he wants you to be through tests. So learn to give thanks for all things. Through the good and also through the bad even things you don't understand. Thank him any how, because through these things God is making you to be your very best.

# 53

## When You're Faithful

─⟨§⟩─

When your faithful the devil will attack. It may be through people you thought you could trust. It may be from loved ones as well as family members. It may be through people in Church. In which ever form he tries to come. He wants you to be unfaithful. He wants you to think what you're doing is not working for you. But that's when you'd better turn to God's word and know whether it's true or not. Whether it comes from a Speaker, a Deacon, a Preacher, a Prophet, or Evangelist, no matter who it comes from. If it doesn't line up with the Word of God, don't let it take hold of your spirit. Take heed to what you listen to and what you intake pay attention. So when you hear something that doesn't line up with the Word of God, you will know that you know if it's from God or man. Know who is talking to you and at you. Is it man or God? That's why you better read God's Word. So that you will know what you know is real or not. For God's word is true, so let God be real and every man a liar. So remember to know that you know who is telling you. And continue to be faithful for God is watching over you. People may hear the rumor; they may even lie on you. But one thing to remember God is keeping record and he's watching over you.

# When You're Going Through: Here's A Poem Just For You

—❧—

When you're going through, here's what to do: Turn to your Bible, there's a scripture just for you. When you feel no one cares, remember Jesus is always there to lead and guide you every step of the way. Because he will bring you joy each and every day. I just thought I'll write this poem to you. To let you know I love you. I appreciate you. And the love you share because you love who I love and his name is always there when we talk. Our conversation is never boring because talking about him, we both get excited. So stay encouraged no matter what you go through. And just look in the mirror if you are ever discouraged and say the word Jesus and watch how your face lights up. And you will never be discouraged or ever dismayed because when you say Jesus, it will lighten up your day.

# *You Can Count On Me*

———⁓ৡ⁓———

When troubles come your way, you can count on me. When you don't know what to say. You can count on me. When people lie on you. You can count on me. When people talk about you. You can count on me. When you feel low in the spirit. You can count on me. When you need encouraging. You can count on me. When you feel depressed. You can count on me. When I say you can count on me, it's not just words, but trust in me and acknowledge me in good times and bad. So when things happen and one day you will go through,. You will have the confidence from times before. You can count on me.

# 56

## People Say They Know Me

—⟐—

You say you know me. Why do you gossip? You say you know me. Why do you try to fake it to make it? You say you know me. Then you pretend to know me. But you don't. You say you know me. But you won't pray for people. You say you know me. But you don't show mercy. Instead of praying for people, you talk about them. You say you know me, but yet you play with my words. You say you know me, but if you had known me, you would know I'm real. You continue to gossip, complain, point fingers; you're not like me. For I have compassion on people. Where is it that you know me, check yourself. Watch your conversation, are they edifying me? If not, you don't know me.

# Being Part Of The Ministry

———⁓ ᔯ ⁓———

How is it that you can say you're Saved? Are in the Choir? Are on th Usher Board? Or the Pastor? Or the Deacon? Or whatever part you're taking in the Ministry? In the choir are you meaning words that you sing? Are you living the life you're singing about? Or being the Treasurer. Are you cheating, are you being honest? And Pastor, are you leading in all faithfulness? Are you saying what people want to hear? Are what thus says the Lord? Or even the Deacon? Are you doing like God says? What a Deacon should be? Check yourself in every area you're holding: is it real? Are you faking it to make it? Be real in whatever you do for God. For he that worships him must worship him in spirit and in truth. God inhabit pure worship and pure praise. Are you real or you fake? Check yourself and see if what you do and even what you say is how God would do it and say it.

# He Who Loves Is Of God

—⚬§⚬—

He who loves is of God. Words are easy to say, but actions show what you mean. For from the abundance of the heart, the mouth speaks. You say you love, and you say you care. Where is the love? I don't see it there, you say you pray for people. You say you have compassion, I don't see it. Where is it there? Don't you know I love you? Don't you know I care when you mistreat people. Even that I see, so be careful what you say. In people's faces; be careful what you say behind their backs, Because one day you just might need that person to pick you up when you're slack.

## Where Is The Peace?

—∽⚬∾—

You say I'm your Father, Where is the peace? You say you know I love you. Where is the peace? You say you trust me. Where is the peace? You say you're in faith. Where is the peace? You say you know I'm real, Where is the peace? Truly if you know me, you would know he who knows me keeps the peace. For my children are known by the peace they keep. Are you keeping peace? Or are you making trouble? Are you doing what I say? Are you starting trouble? Check yourself and see if it's you who is starting trouble. Because I'm known by peace. In any situation you may face or see. Where is the peace.

# In Time Of Crisis

In time of a crisis, sometimes it's hard. But I know if I trust in God, he won't leave me alone. Sometimes the pain hurts so deep. But even in the mist he keeps me at peace. Sometimes I cry, sometimes I feel bad. But in all, I trust God because I now he's there. People may not understand why I'm always the same, Because as long as I stay before God, he let's me know he's there. My God (Jesus), the Father, and Precious Holy Spirit. They are always with me. When I cry, when I hurt, or when I need to feel at peace. I love them very much because no matter what I go through, I always know they are near to keep me where I need to be. So the next time you're going through. Always know God will be there for you in times of trouble. He'll keep you in peace.

# Bless Your Children (Part One)

Be careful what you say to your children so that you don't hurt or curse them instead of blessing them. Because what you say might scare them if it's not positive. Let them know you're there so that they will feel comfortable to tell you things that go on in their lives. Sometimes they look at you sadly, and you don't even notice. Their hearts hurt sometime because of things they go through. Sometimes they can't help the things they go through. But as a parent, it's our job to make sure everything is all right. We have to speak life over our children. We have to bless them when we're going through. We have to bless them when everything is fine, But we need to bless them at all times. Even when they don't listen. Even when they do listen. But just remember one valuable thing; Never say negatives to your child. That will scare or that could hurt that can make a different in life or death. That would even make them bitter in their spirit. So speak positively and they will always remember that even in times when they look back.

# 62

## *Bless Your Children (Part Two)*

In my words, I say train up a child in the way he should go and when he is old, he will not depart. I also say bless and curse not. Why do you speak bitterly to them? Why do you hurt them with words that you don't even mean? You say negative things out of anger. Not realizing that your bruising your child. They go to their rooms, they even cry to me. You don't seem to see what they feel in the things that you say. Sometimes they want to do what's right; Sometimes they don't. But make sure your speaking all the right things. So that your blessing even when your hurt. But you must remember they are the ones who must come first. They are your future generation. You must bless them. So that they will lead the way. There will be a time when they are older. And what you do and say will play a part in how they end up. So bless your children with all of your heart. Bless them with all of your might. For one day you will be glad because it will all pay off.

# 63

## What Jesus Means To Me

—⁓§⁓—

Jesus, you are to me more than words could ever say: You mean so much to me. They don't have a word that could say what you are to me. Because you mean so much to me. When I was in the world, I messed up several times, but still you loved me. When I was lost, you found me. You showed me what life could be indeed. All I had to do was trust you. And you delivered me. You brought me out of darkness into your marvelous light, And now I'm Saved, yes indeed. I am Saved!. I am Saved! Yes indeed!

# 64

## *When You're Feeling Down And Blue*

―⚹―

When you feeling down and blue and you don't know what to do. Just remember Jesus loves and cares for you. See it's not by chance I came your way. But God had a plan for us today. See, he wants you to see his love through me, and the realness you can be when you serve him. You don't have to be a fake. You can be real day by day. But you just have to let God lead your way. So when your feeling down and blue and don't know what to do. Just take a look at me and see the joy I have by me serving Jesus. Who will also bring you through. So never be afraid to ask for prayer or even a word of encouragement. For it's not by chance I came down your path. He heals the broken in heart and binds up their wounds.

# 65

## Faith

—⟋ঞ⟍—

Faith is truly the substance of things hoped, for the evidence of things not seen. If you see it why yet hope for it. But we hope for it by faith and then we, with patience, wait for it. When your in faith you do something. You act in faith by doing something. You have to put faith to work. God says in his word faith without work is dead. That is so because if we say we believe God for something and we never act on what we're believing him for nothing will happen. But if you act on what you're believing. God will back us up. He will prove himself to be faithful. We just got to show God that we will do something and just keep thanking him for what we're asking him for. And then and then only will he back us up. Because God will do his part. But we also have to do something first by acting upon what we're believing God for, and that is faith.

## 66

### Don't Label Me-Pray For Me

—⚬§⚬—

So many times people look for fault in each other. Not realizing they have something wrong with them as well. If you pray for one another, you wouldn't have time to talk about them. Why can't you love as God loves you? Where is the love, you should have for another. Why can't you pray for your neighbors, instead of pointing your finger? Instead of labeling your neighbors, as he's a drug dealer, he's a liar, a thief, a gossiper, a cheater, he curses too much; pray for him, you wasn't always the way you are. Even in Titus in the Bible, reading the Chapter3 Verses2-5 God say to speak no evil of no man to be. But gentle showing all meekness toward all men. For we ourselves also were sometimes foolish, disobedient, deceived, serving divers lust and pleasures. Living in malice and envy hateful and hating one another. But after that, the kindness and love of God, our Saviour toward man appeared. Not by works of righteousness which we have done, but according to his mercy, he Saved us. By the washing of regeneration and renewing of the Holy Ghost. So why can't you pray for one another instead of pointing your finger? For all have sinned and come short of the Glory of God. So remember the next time you get ready to label someone, don't label him pray for him. Or just hush! If you can't say something to build someone up, Don't say something to tear them down. Amen

67

## Why Do I Go To Church?

———⚬§⚬———

The reason I go to Church: God word says we're suppose to assemble ourselves among the saints. God says we're suppose to come before his presence with singing. We're suppose to enter into his courts with praise. We're suppose to love one another. We're suppose to greet each other. We're suppose to love the things God loves. We're suppose to lift up Holy hands before the Lord. And most of all, we're suppose to love to go. Because we're suppose to love what God loves and God loves his Church. Thank you Holy Ghost. Amen

# Never Worry About How People Look At You When You Praise God

~ ⚘ ~

When you praise God. It's and individual thing. It is between you and God, so never worry when people stare at you. For you know why you are there. You come to Church to praise God and hear his word. Church should be the place where you are set free and praise is one of the weapons to get deliverance. So if someone ever looks at you when you praising God, or even ask you why you praise so hard, say because Church is the one place where you can be freed. And this why I praise him so because he unlocks doors that's closed against me.

## *Having Joy Within*

~⚬§⚬~

In life there's so many trials, but in them all. I'm still thankful to God. I know if you don't have tests you will never have a testimony. But in them all I'm learning more and more that I need Jesus, I can't make it in this world without him. He's the only one that never changes. He's the only one that will never leave you. Though trials of life compass me about, but still I know God will see me out. I know the devil would love for me to write a negative, but in it all there's nothing negative to say. Because deep down I have joy unspeakable joy. That has been bestowed on me for such a time as this. And when it's down on the inside nothing or no one can take it away. Whether trial, test, tribulation, anguish, suffering, even things you just can't explain or understand. You just can't seem to understand, but through it all you still smile beneath, because it's on the inside. And nothing can take it away, for it's deep down within, And that's why I can truly say the joy of Lord is truly my strength and his joy is what keeps me.

# Through Pain And Suffering, I Will Still Trust Jesus

When going through life and tests come your way, sometimes it's hard, sometimes you may feel it's got you. But you know God will deliver you. You have the faith because of times before When tests come your way, you look back and think when you were going through before. God, unlock those doors. But sometimes tests come your way, and the pain seems to be unbearable, because you keep doing right. You even begin to check yourself. Am I reading? Am I studying? Am I fasting? Am I and a doer of the word as well as a hearer? And after checking yourself through it all. You feel no conviction of having done anything wrong, then you say, Well I must be tried, I must be tested, and I know through it all God will help me. But you wonder because it hurts so bad. But then it comes up from deep within. If Jesus suffered on the cross for us, we must also suffer for him. You say But I haven't done anything wrong. But neither did he, but you just got to keep your hand in Jesus hand, For he knows just why things are happening at this time. But he loves you and will deliver you through,. For he says many are the afflictions of the righteous, but the Lord delivereth them out of them all. So you know he will see you through. So keep your hand in Jesus hand, and keep the faith, and keep trusting him. For he will see you through, and he will stop the pain that keeps hurting you.

# Christmas Should Be Every Day To The Saints

〜⑨〜

If you look at the world, they get ready for one day in a year. And that one day means a lot to them. Well this the way it should be for the Saints. Listen and listen good: Christmas to the Saints should be giving Christ year around. Christmas to the Saints should be helping someone out. Christmas to the Saints is letting someone know you will always be there. These are just a few, but if I was to write a list, as in some people make a list of what they want for Christmas. The list would never end. Because to do good should never end. God says we should never get weary in well doing because we will reap if we faint not. So we are blessed year round. We are always receiving gifts from the Lord and having Jesus Christ, the son of God, is the greatest gift anyone could have. So share him yearly not just on certain occasions. Because to give Christ to someone your gifts will come daily. Because Jesus will bless you for all that you do. So when someone asks you about Christmas, say Christmas is daily.

# Knowing Who You Are

I was sitting in my bedroom and talking to the Lord, and just looking back over my life and realizing for the first time in my life I actually knew what I wanted in life and who I am. I want to be a power ball for the Lord. I want to be a powerful woman of God. I don't want to be a doctor, a lawyer, or nurse or teacher. I just want to be used by God and to please God so that one day when I stand before him, he will say unto me it's finished. Well done thy good and faithful servant. That is my desire is to please God and do his will and now I know. Amen. I love you God, the Father, the Son and Precious Holy Ghost. Amen. Also when I was growing up and in school when they asked me what I wanted to be, I never knew what I wanted to be and that was because Jesus had his plan for my life to use me for his purpose. And for the first time in my life. I'm happy and I'm stable: not confused and proud to be a child of God. And for the first time. I know what I want out of life, who I am, and who, I belong to, and his name is Jesus Christ the Son of God. Thank you God, for letting me know who I am.

# Mothers Through Trials and Testing

—⟋§⟍—

There are many things that women go through in general, but one thing when you know the Lord, you know he will see you through. But another thing is when you don't you really don't know what to do. In life there are many things you're going to go through. Many trials and many test but what is best is when you know the Lord. He sustains you through whatever you go through. But when you don't know the Lord, you feel there's no help. Then you began to do things that is even abominable even to yourself. You can end up with many afflictions, than what the situation at hand really is, you don't know. Even in God word, he tells us in the world there will be tribulation, but be of good cheer. He tell us that he over come the world and so can we. But if you don't know Jesus, how can you know you are an over comer. If you don't know him who helps you overcome? So as I finish up this reading, I pray in Jesus name, If there is a mother or anyone out there that may be going through something and all hope is gone. I want to introduce you to my friend, Jesus who can help you to make it on. He will never leave you or ever forsake you. People you trust may hurt you and people you depend on might disappoint you or even let you down, but my friend Jesus will always be around. He won't treat you like people. He'll never do you wrong. He'll never lie on you. Or even cause you to hurt, but he will do you good and not evil all the days of your life. Make him number in your life, so when trials and test come you won't flip out or get discouraged. Or dismayed or even want to commit suicide. If you make him number one in your life, You will have peace each and every day of your life for the rest of your life.

# Remembering How I Use To Be

———◦§◦———

I look at me and looking back over my life, and I'm not like I use to be. The things I use to do I don't want to do anymore. The places I use to go I don't want to go no more. The clothes I use to wear, I don't want to wear no more. The desires I use to have, I don't have no more. When Jesus came into my life, he changed everything in me. The thought, the feelings. He changed me completely. He didn't half do anything. But he cleaned me completely up. You see Jesus is a clean God, very clean and when he clean you up you won't go back no more. You want get dirty no more unless you choose to. God is working it out for you so you got to know God don't half do know job. You are not cleaned until God completely cleans you up. So allow God to finish you up and you won't ever get dirty again. Unless you choose to go back into the world.

# The Peace Of God How You Know You Got It: Examine Yourself

—⟶⟨§⟩⟵—

Peace, when you go to the hospital for one thing and find out you got another.

Peace, When you can work a job and smile with people and mean it when you know they have done you wrong. Peace When you know someone have done you wrong and you see them going through for doing you wrong and you have compassion for them. And you feel sorry that they are going through. Even though they done you wrong. Peace When you are angry, but yet you still are maintaining your integrity in the situation you're going through. Why you are talking about it. Peace. Someone you work with, you pray and fast with, makes you look bad in front of the supervisor and you thought they meant you good. Peace. When you can smile when trouble is all around you, test after test, month after month, after month, Peace. When you can go out and witness to someone else. When you yourself have found out some terrible news about yourself that involves your loved one. Peace, when you know someone doesn't like you, but you can still smile at them, but you mean it from your heart. Peace, when people have done you wrong, lie on you, talked about you, mistreated you, and you can still call their name out in prayer for good. Peace. And to sum it all up, peace is only something God can give because when you don't have the peace of God in all these situations I have named, you will probably be done flipped out, killed somebody, done evil for evil, figuring out a way to pay back, had an affair yourself, lied back on someone, make someone look bad, and you would have figured out a way to get even. But when you have the peace of God, even though it hurts, you cry and you don't understand how you are handling it. Like you even begin to wonder if something is wrong with you. Or even if you're in denial, but in it all you just keep on smiling, for the smile on your face wipes away all the shame and you keep looking toward the hills, which cometh your help and your help cometh from the Lord. So may the peace God gives you keep you, and only the children of God have this peace. So if you have been in any of these situations, and you know you didn't have this kind of peace. Ask God to save you first and then ask him to give you his peace that surpasses all understanding. And then and then only will you be able to smile with a real smile. When going through a test, for then you will know you have the peace of God because of how you handle these trials. This is peace.

# 76

## Total Dependency On God

———❦———

God wants us to put our total trust in him. In good times as well as bad. When we are being tested. God is teaching us through those tests how to depend on him. How can you say you can depend on God, if you never had to depend on him to know you could? God is not trying to hurt you when you are going through a test. But he wants you to learn how to lean and depend on him. He wants you to acknowledge him in all your ways. And for you not to lean on your own understanding. So next time you're faced with at trail and with a test, remember God want you to lean and depend on him in every test.

# Keeping Your Mind On Jesus

—⟶৯⟵—

God word say he will keep you in perfect peace when your mind is stayed on him. If you keep God in your thoughts and on your mind, you wouldn't worry. You wouldn't be dismayed, for the name of Jesus will bring peace in every way. So next time you're faced with a trial or with a test, remember to keep your mind on Jesus and he will make you forget about the test, for he will give you a different frame of mind for looking at that test and at that situation. For God knows how to fix every situation.

# 78

## *Never Ashaming God's Name*

—◦⑤◦—

Sometimes you will have a test that requires you to hold your peace. You may be able to retaliate, but you sometimes have to hold your peace, for it's not about your name that you are shaming. But it's God's name. When you carry the name of being a Christian, you represent God. So it's not about you only. So when people try to upset you, never let them dictate how you act. Remember you represent Jesus Christ. The Son of God. And that should make you feel you can go through you can take what ever your going through to keep from shaming the name of Christ.

# 79

## God Got His Eye On You

—◈—

God is watching you. He sees everything you say and do. You may feel no one sees you but God does. It shouldn't be a matter of people watching you or not. For God is the one who makes the difference. People can't place you in heaven or hell. So you shouldn't worry about people seeing you. You should worry about God watching you. So the next time you are alone and feel no one is watching you remember God got his eye on you. And he sees everything you do.

# 80

## There's Nothing Wrong With Loving Jesus

Jesus is the best thing that could have ever happen to me. I don't worry, I don't have to be afraid, I don't have to be dismayed. When trouble comes my way, I know what to do is pray. For God loves and cares for me. For it is he that set me free. How can I not love him? It's because of him I have a new life. I love him so, and that's true there's nothing wrong with loving him so. He's my life and my salvation. He's my God in him whom I trust, and I will forever love him, for there's nothing wrong with loving him so.

# 81

## *Wait On God*

———⚬§⚬———

After you have prayed, wait. After you have fasted, wait. After you're done reading God's word, wait, After you have done what the Lord said to do, all you can do is wait, wait. You have to have patience with God. God's timing is not our timing, but he is never late. He's always on time. You just have to keep your hand in God's hand, and wait for change to come. Be thankful while waiting. Keep doing what you've been doing: going to Church, Prayer, Bible Study, both services on Sunday. And then only will change come. You just have to wait, wait. For God will come if you wait.

# God Is Real

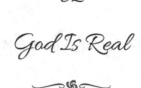

God is real. He so real to me. If you can feel what I feel, and see what I see. I feel his presence when I go to the grocery store. I can feel his presence when I am driving down the street. I can feel his presence when I am at work. I can feel his presence everywhere I go. He will show up at anytime, and that I know. He's so real to me I know he's always with me. When I go out, he's with me. When I come in, he's with me. He protects me where I go My God, he's always with me that I know.

# Make God Number One

Make God number one in your life, And he will always guide and protect you through life. God doesn't want to be second, he wants your very best. So make him number one, So when trials and test come, you will be able to stand. For God will be number one. We all need to make him number one. Because when test and trial come. You will know where your faith and hope and confidence is base on who you made number one.

# 84

## Don't Let No One Hinder Your Walk With God

~◈~

Don't let know one hinder your walk with God. See it's not about that person, it's about the devil messing up your relationship with God. He know s if he can get someone to make you sin. He know he has you where he wants you and always remember it's not people that are coming against you, but the devil wants to use them to get next to you. Don't fall for his tricks. Don't fall for his tempt, for all the devil want is to get you to mess up. Don't let no one hinder your walk with God. For no one can ever make you fall. Keep your faith and trust in God.

# Having The Desire Of The Things Of God

When you read God's word, you should want the things God said you could have. God's words shows what he likes. You have to read to find out what he likes. God can give you his promises, but how can you know what they are if you don't read to know? You should take part in all God's interest. If God says love, you should love. If God says have mercy, have mercy. If God says have compassion, have compassion. If God says love your neighbor as yourself, you should. You should love what God loves. You should take interest in what God loves. You should desire the things that God loves. Having the desire of the things God loves. And mostly you should love people because that is what God truly loves. He is concerned about the souls of people.

# 86

## You Can Be Free From Sin

—⟨φ⟩—

You can be free from sin if you let God help you within. There's nothing too hard for God. You just got to want to stop. God won't force himself on you. He gives you a choice if you want to stop. Sin is something that you got to want to stop. For God can't help you if you don't want to stop. God is so good he gives you a choice in all that you do. So if you want to be free from sin, you have to ask God to help you within. You have to get Saved first, and that's when you can begin to get free.

## *Forgive and Forget And Go On*

~ঌ~

It's not always easy to forget, but with God all things are possible. You have to forgive and forget and go on. For that thing that comes to you will keep carrying on. The devil wants you to keep remembering so you will keep bitterness in your heart. He wants you to think you didn't get delivered from the start. But if God delivers you that is all that matters. The devil is a liar. Don't ever feel you haven't been deliver. He just wants to keep bringing it back to your remembrance. Remember, if you going through a trial or a test and after you have been delivered just let it rest. Even if the devil tries to remind you what happened just remember to for give and forget and go on.

# All Things Work Together For them Who Love the Lord

❦

You may be faced with tests and maybe faced with trials. But God will always help you out. There's no defeats planned for your life. You just have to remember God will bring you out. For all things work together for good for those who love the Lord. If God is the love of your life remember you don't have to fight. For the battle is not yours, it's the Lord. So cast all your cares on him for he cares for you. And know good thing will be withheld from them who love the Lord. So remember there's only good things planned for those who love the Lord and read God's word, and then you will know.

# 89

## *After The Test Comes The Blessing*

~⚬~

Even Job when he was tested. When he came out he received God's blessing. When you go through a test, there's reward after it's finished. God will reward you all you have been through. After you have endured you will be rewarded. You have to know God is for you. It is good that you have been afflicted to know that God is with you. How will you know if God is with you. If you don't have test to show you God is with you.? It's through testing you know God is for you. It's through trial is you know you're not alone. So when you are tested, remember after it's over, you will receive the blessing.

# 90

## *What You Going To Do When You're Left Alone*

—◦⟨§⟩◦—

People may like you as long as you agree with them. But what are you going to do when you don't agree with them? You must know to put God first so, if people leave you alone you will know God is for you. Never feel your alone even if people don't acknowledge you are around. For God will always be with you, even to the end of the world. So if people stop coming around you, or people stop calling you, or if people don't seem to care for you make sure your ankle is in the Lord. And then you won't ever feel alone. Even if people are not around, you will know God is always around. And you are never left alone. For if God is with you, you will never be alone.

# 91

## I Learned How To Walk Without Man And I Learned How To Walk With God

————— ✥ —————

You come to a point in your walk with God where he teaches you total dependence on him and not on man. See, you can put your trust in man, and he will fell you. But if you put your trust in God, he will see you through. See if you put your trust in man and if they hurt you, you may get mad at God. But if you put your trust in God, and if man hurt you, you know God will deliver you. God allow you to go through test and trials so you can learn how to depend on him not on man. Through test is when you learn how to depend on God, for when there's nothing man can do, you know it's up to God to see you through. So when trouble come you won't have to worry. You know it's God who will see you through, so walk with God and not with man. For it's God who hold the whole world in his hand.

# Whatever You're Going Through, God Is Working Something Out In You

―⟨§⟩―

Whatever your faced with God allowed it to come to strengthen you when you're Saved. God has planned no defeats for your life. He's working things out in your life. You may not understand the trials. But in it all God is working it out some how. God is making you through what you go through. He's molding and shaping you in your test. Because when you come out you are made to be the best. For you will act better after your test. You will be more humble after a test. You will be more understanding after a test. And most of, you will know just how to handle the devil when he comes to mess with you with the same tempt again.

# Seek Ye First The Kingdom Of God

There are many things we may want out of life. But we must first seek God and all his righteousness shall be added unto us. God knows our needs. He also knows our wants. But there's also something we must do for us to get what we want: We must seek God, face night and day. We must pray in order to make it. The world will sell us a counterfeit, but what God gives us is everlasting and is real. So when we think about the things we want, we need to turn our Bible to Psalm 37:4 And its says,: Delight yourself in the Lord and he will give you the desires of your heart so there's something we must first do." We got to love the Lord with all our heart and all our soul. We must put God first before everything. And then and then only will we get those things that we desire the most.

# When I'm In Test

When I'm in trouble, all I have to do is call on the Lord. For he will answer prayer. For I know he's always there. Next time I'm going through I know just what to do. I'll call on the Lord, I know he will help me through. I know he will be there. I know he will answer prayer. The test of life sometimes passes me by. And even then I know God will be right there. Sometimes I know it's hard, the test seems so hard, but Jesus will be right there. Next time I go through. I'll always know what to do. Next time I go through, I now just what to do. Jesus will see me through. I know he will be right there. For I know he will answer my prayer. For I know he's there, and I know he will answer my prayer, for he will see me through.

# 95

## I'm A Fanatic For God

Has there ever been something that you just love to do? Has there ever been a place you love to go? Or even something you just love. Well for me, I speak in respect of my love for God. I love God with all my heart. And with all my soul, I love him with my being and everything within me. To talk about him, I get excited. To tell of his goodness, I'm thrilled. Just to love him it makes me to smile. Oh I love Jesus with all my heart. He's my comforter, he is my healer, he's my deliverer, he's my way maker. He's my joy and my strength. And most of all, he is my God. And that's why I'm a fanatic for Jesus. For he is my all in all. And there's no one who can ever take his place, no not at all.

# 96

## The Children Are Our Future

~⚬~

The children are our future. We must tell them God's word and tell them about Jesus, that he is God's son. We must tell them about our Lord, that he is God. We must let them know God loves them. And remind them that Jesus is the way And tell them so that they will know the way. I'm so glad the Lord chose me, for his Shaconner Glory. I'm so glad I am his child. I know he kept me for his purpose. I won't turn, oh no I won't. As long as God is guiding me, I know the Lord is God and that he is mine. Because he choose me for his purpose. I know I belong to God and he is my Saviour. Yes, I know people looking for something, but they don't know God is the answer. They don't know he's real for they never tried him. All you have to do is give Jesus a chance to show you he's Lord of Lord and King of Kings. Then you'll know. He's the most honorable Lord of Lords and King of Kings. All you have to do is believe in him, then you will see he's Lord. He's the most awesome Lord of Lords, and King of Kings. He's the most glorious Lord of Lords, and King of Kings. And this I know.

## *Words Of Encouragement*

—◦§◦—

Look unto the hills whence cometh your help, your help cometh from the Lord. He will not let your foot be removed. He that keepeth thee neither slumber nor sleep. So though you feel sad deep within, God will comfort you from within. For he sees your tears, he know your cries, he knows your heart and he will deliver. For he is the answer. God will comfort and see you through, put your hands in his hands and he will lift you up. For he says many are the afflictions of the righteous, but the Lord delivereth him out of them all. So though you just don't understand, but keep your hands in God's hands for he knows why things happen the way they do. But he loves you and he will see you through. So trust the Lord with all your heart, and he will sustain you and see you through. Jesus loves you and he will be with you. So keep the faith and keep trusting God. For he will see you through and he will also make away for you, too. So that you can do the things that you need to do.

# Why Are You Still Struggling After You Passed The Test?

Why are you still struggling
After you passed the test?

Why are you still worrying after God's words said he would keep you in perfect peace whose mind is stayed on him? Why are you still struggling, when God said no weapons formed against you shall prosper? Why are you still struggling when all things work together for good for them who love the Lord? You no longer have to struggle when going through a test. All you have to do is read God's word and there's a scripture in God's word for every test you have. All you have to do is read God's word to know what he says, and you will know you have already passed the test.

## 99

# The Anointing Comes Through Test

When you say Lord, bless me with more anointing, what you are really saying is Lord, send more trials in my life. How the anointing comes is through test. Without tests, you can't have the anointing. Because the anointing comes to destroy the yoke of bondage and unless your in a test how can you be in bondage. You have to be going through something in order to be in a test. But what ever test you go through. God won't put no more on you than you can bear. He knows what you can take and what you can't so be thankful for test and trials for the anointing will destroy the yoke of bondage. And God will work it out for you somehow.

# Hold On 'Till Your Change Come

Don't give up, though it hurts. Don't give up, though it's pain. Hold on and wait for change. Change will come if you wait on the Lord. Troubles don't last always neither do tests. You just have to be patience and wait on God. For he sees what you go through, and he knows what hurt you. He will deliver you. But you must hold on and wait on him. Through trials and test seem to get you down. Don't stop holding on and waiting on God. For he will come soon and you just have to be calm and wait on him. And he will see you through.

# 101

## When You Find Someone Strong In The Lord They Have Been Through Something

———⟡———

When you see men and women of God who are powerful in the Lord. They have been through something. It's not by chance they have what they have. It's through trials and test God makes you be your very best. You're broken in spirt at times; you have much pain in your heart at times; it's through tribulation, hurts, and pain God gives you a name. He allows you to go through so that he will get the 'Glory in how he delivers you. That's why it's important to give your testimony to let people know. How God delivered you and from where he brought you. So when ever you hear someone say he is powerful in the Lord, remember, it's through tests God makes you to be what he wants you to be through test.

# 102

## Sharing Is Caring

—⟶⟨§⟩⟵—

When you give someone Jesus your showing you care when you tell them he Saves you sharing them hope. Although they don't seem to know, you must love them. Because to share Jesus with someone is just the beginning. Because once they begin to know him, they will see you care. To share Jesus with someone is more precious than rubies. To share Jesus with someone is more precious than gold. Money can never take the place of telling someone he Saves. You may not have silver to give them. You may not have gold, but if you share Jesus with someone, that is all they will need to know. The rubies will come and even the gold and everything else too. Because he is the one who can bring all those things to you. So share Jesus with someone. Let them know he cares. Because had not someone told you about him, you would not even be here.

# 103

## *People You Think You Can Trust*

———⚬§⚬———

When you put your trust in man, they will fail you. When you put your trust in a friend, he will hurt you. People you think you know and people you think know you, sometimes are the ones that hurts you. You treat them nicely, you be kind to them. You check on them, and you see about them, But when trouble comes their way, they so easily forget how good you have been to them, You try to say things to make them feel good. You try to say things to encourage them. You try to say things to make it better, but still in all thy hurt you. That's why you need to make God your friend. For he won't treat you like man. He will never hurt you, he will never deceive you. He will never think falsely of you because truly he will know you.

# 104

## You Better Put Your Trust In God Because Before It's Over, You're Going To Wish You Had

—⟨§⟩—

You put your trust in man, they will fail you. You put your confidence in many things, they will disappoint you. You think you know someone, yet he hurts you. You don't think someone who you thought you knew would hurt you. You need to put your trust in God. Because, before it's over, you're going to wish you had before. Because people will hurt, fail, disappoint you. But through it all. God is still faithful to deliver you. Even though you didn't put your trust in getting to know him.

# 105

## Jesus Is The Only One Who Can Give You Happiness In This Life

———⁘———

Real happiness comes from God. You may say, well I'm happy. I'm glad, I'm doing well. Happiness and joy in God is when you have bills due and you don't have the money, but you're still smiling. Happiness is when you lost a loved one. And you can still smile. Happiness is when you get mistreated on your job. Yet your still smiling. Happiness is when you've done right by people. And you're still mistreated. That's real happiness and much, much more can be named. But real complete happiness can only come from God. Because know matter what you're going through, you're still smiling. Only God can give you that kind of happiness. Because the joy of the Lord can be the only thing that can strengthen you. In good times as well as bad. And that's true happiness. And that only can come from God.

I can write thru experiences I have been through in my life. I have written these, poems through pain, gladness, joy, feeling alone, through many things I have been through, and experiences I have faced, and things the Lord put in my spirit to write about. For I couldn't write any of these poems, and readings had not I been there. Or the Lord had not given them to me. I thank God for allowing me to hurt, to go through all the tests and not understanding, but I thank him. I didn't complain or charge him foolishly for my testing, It was good I was afflicted that I might know God and know he cares for me. I love Jesus and he is really the head of my life. He is my Saviour,. He is the love of my life, and my total dependency is on him. He has taught me through tests and trials how to put my total dependency on him and that's what God wants us to do is to depend totally on him. In every situation, in everything we go through he wants us to depend on him and to trust him. For he cares, he really does, and he really loves us, and he has planned no defeats for our life. So remember all the days of your life that Jesus cares he really do. And whatever you go through God will always be there for you. Finally, I would like to thank Jesus for giving me a mind to write all these poems and reading. It's God who gets the glory for this book. Thank you Jesus, God the Father and Precious Holy Spirit.

Amen.
By: Bren Daniels
Jesus, The Writer